STAR WARS
THE UNAUTHORIZED
TRIVIA BOOK

LITTLE BOOKS ABOUT BIG THINGS

STAR WARS
THE UNAUTHORIZED TRIVIA BOOK

DAMON BROWN

FALL RIVER PRESS

New York

FALL RIVER PRESS

New York

An Imprint of Sterling Publishing
387 Park Avenue South
New York, NY 10016

Cover design by Igor Satanovsky
Book design by Michele L. Trombley

ISBN 978-1-4351-4669-3

Distributed in Canada by Sterling Publishing
c/o Canadian Manda Group, 165 Dufferin Street
Toronto, Ontario, Canada M6K 3H6
Distributed in the United Kingdom by GMC Distribution Services
Castle Place, 166 High Street, Lewes, East Sussex, England BN7 1XU
Distributed in Australia by Capricorn Link (Australia) Pty. Ltd.
P.O. Box 704, Windsor, NSW 2756, Australia

For information about custom editions, special sales, and premium and
corporate purchases, please contact Sterling Special Sales at
800-805-5489 or specialsales@sterlingpublishing.com.

Manufactured in Canada

2 4 6 8 10 9 7 5 3 1

www.sterlingpublishing.com

INTRODUCTION

Star Wars is easily the most controversial mainstream movie series of all time. This is not because it borrows liberally from the Japanese film *The Hidden Fortress*, or because it launched the obscenely lucrative Hollywood toy tie-in industry. Star Wars is controversial because George Lucas, the crazy genius who created our beloved story, has no problem revising the series. He considers the Star Wars galaxy an unfinished painting; something to be tweaked, adjusted, and, in some cases, reduced.

The very book of trivia you have in your hands may help us understand the world of Star Wars and, as a result, George Lucas himself. This is more than a bunch of facts. The collective anecdotes, quotes, and ideas are a roadmap to seeing what inspired Lucas, why the characters stay with us, and how Star Wars has influenced all of our lives.

Damon Brown
February 2013

Note: For the sake of simplicity, the series' first film to be released in theaters, *Star Wars Episode IV: A New Hope*, is sometimes referred to simply as *Star Wars*.

The end of George Lucas' directorial debut, the existential 1971 science-fiction film *THX 1138*, provides a brief glimpse at some odd hairy creatures. Warner Bros. reportedly hated the film but loved the cute guys making a cameo before the credits. Lucas decided to include them in his next sci-fi effort, *Star Wars*, and he named them Wookies.

TRUE OR FALSE?

Luke Skywalker's original name was Luke Starkiller.

TRUE.

One of the earliest *Star Wars* drafts was reportedly called "Adventures of Luke Starkiller, as Taken from the Journal of the Whills, Saga I: The Star Wars."

George Lucas modeled the infamous Emperor Palpatine after U.S. president Richard Nixon. Lucas finalized the *Star Wars* manuscript in summer 1975, a year after Nixon's resignation following the Watergate trial. Some critics, however, believe Lucas claimed the Nixon inspiration after the fact, hoping it would draw more people to see *Star Wars*.

Star Wars action figures are still a multimillion-dollar business today, but they became extremely popular as soon as the original *Star Wars* hit the screen decades ago. They were in such demand in 1977 that toy company Kenner stuck rain checks in empty boxes so kids could have their figures shipped to them later!

In 1978, Lucas worked with CBS to create the now-infamous *Star Wars Holiday Special*. Centered around Chewbacca looking for his family, the two-hour TV movie was a monumentally cheesy misfire. Realizing his error, Lucas reportedly hunted down as many copies as possible so it wouldn't be seen again. He's lucky it was made before the Internet existed, although some grainy footage can still be found online.

250,000,000

The approximate number of
Star Wars figures sold from
1978 to 1986 alone.

$172,000

The amount that a model of
Chewbacca's head, used in the
first *Star Wars* trilogy, sold
for at a 2012 auction.

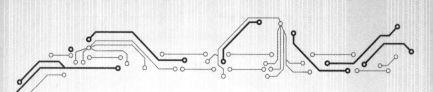

QUESTION:

Legendary puppeteer Frank Oz gave Yoda his distinctive speaking style, but he also did the voice for what other iconic 1970s puppet?

- a. Lamb Chop
- b. Miss Piggy
- c. All the Banana Splits
- d. Morris the Cat

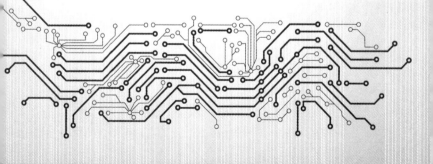

ANSWER:

b. Miss Piggy

Frank Oz voiced fellow Muppet Fozzie Bear too. A longtime collaborator with Jim Henson, Oz directed his own movies, including the camp musical *Little Shop of Horrors* and the comedy *Dirty Rotten Scoundrels*.

⋙ 30 ⋘

The total number of months
George Lucas spent on the
original *Star Wars* script.

⋙ 66 cm ⋘

Yoda's height,
just over 2 feet.

Before the *Star Wars* premiere, George Lucas believed his friend Steven Spielberg's next movie, *Close Encounters of the Third Kind*, would be much more financially successful than his own space epic. Spielberg's film—which opened in November 1977, six months after *Star Wars*—was a smash hit, taking in more than $300 million at the box office.

However, that total was still just a fraction of the first *Star Wars* film's haul, and much less than the entire series it spawned. Spielberg worked with Lucas' breakout star, Harrison Ford, on his next hit film, 1981's *Raiders of the Lost Ark*, which Lucas produced.

George Lucas and his then-wife, Marcia, were convinced *Star Wars* was going to bomb, so they planned on leaving the country during its May 1977 premiere. They mixed up the dates, though, and saw firsthand the long lines of eager moviegoers trying to get in to frequently sold-out screenings. The film earned over $1.5 million in its first weekend—more than 10 percent of what it cost to make.

TRUE OR FALSE?

In episodes IV though VI, C-3PO is never shown walking up or down stairs.

TRUE.

In the first trilogy, the C-3PO suit was too cumbersome to allow actor Anthony Daniels any vertical movement. The editors had to cut around stair sequences to make it look like C-3PO had climbed them.

Well before Internet film clips became available, the 1998 trailer for *Star Wars Episode I: The Phantom Menace* was considered an event. To see it, however, fans had to buy tickets for another film. Screenings for films like *The Siege*, *Meet Joe Black*, and *The Waterboy* were reportedly filled with hardcore fanboys and -girls who left once *The Phantom Menace* trailer was finished. This may have helped goose ticket sales for *Meet Joe Black*, which had received a lukewarm critical and audience response.

Star Wars Episode V: The Empire Strikes Back begins on the ice planet Hoth. In real life, the crew filmed it in wintry Norway around the spectacular Hardangerjøkulen glacier. During the first day of filming, it was 20 degrees below zero Fahrenheit. Because of the extreme temperatures, the crew could shoot for just a few minutes before running back inside to warm up. Some shoots were cut short because the crew's Norwegian guides made them quit early so that whiteout conditions wouldn't keep them from finding their way back to the hotel.

Lucas' script for the original *Star Wars* weighed in at 200 pages, shorter than the average book. The problem? A manuscript page is usually equal to a minute in the final movie, meaning that *Star Wars Episode IV: A New Hope* would have been more than three hours long! Lucas immediately recognized the problem—after all, he had already done the cult film *THX 1138* and the mainstream hit *American Graffiti*—and used just the first act to create *Star Wars*.

Believe it or not, in the original manuscript the infamous Death Star didn't show up, much less explode, until after the first act. Lucas moved the Death Star sequence into *Star Wars* to create a climax to the now-abbreviated manuscript. The theatrical version of *Star Wars Episode IV: A New Hope* is just over two hours long, as are *Episode V: The Empire Strikes Back* and *Episode VI: The Return of the Jedi*. The remastered home versions add a few minutes of bonus footage.

Serials like *Flash Gordon* inspired *Star Wars*, but the biggest literary inspiration may have been Edgar Rice Burroughs' *Barsoom* series, specifically the sci-fi book *A Princess of Mars*. The 1912 title featured a hero, John Carter, navigating his way around a strange, somewhat scary planet while protecting the princess of an alien tribe.

Critics have noted that Lucas not only liked the foreign, otherworldly descriptions in the *Barsoom* series, but arguably used terminology from the century-old book too. For example, Burroughs called lords "jeds," which was likely the origin of the Star Wars term "Jedi." Unfortunately, Star Wars fans didn't support the latest adaptation, Disney's 2012 film *John Carter*. The $200 million movie foundered at the box office.

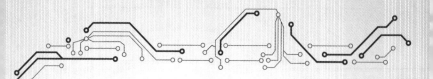

QUESTION:

What are Darth Vader's last words?

a. "You have already saved my life."

b. "Noooooooooooooooooo!"

c. "Tell your sister you were right."

d. "Luke, I am your father."

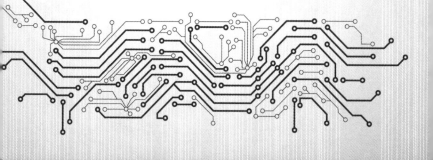

ANSWER:

c. "Tell your sister you were right."

In this scene from *Star Wars Episode VI: The Return of the Jedi*, Darth Vader has just been defeated in a climactic lightsaber duel with his son, Luke, while the Emperor looks on and laughs. Knowing that his father is dying, Luke says, "I've got to save you," to which Vader responds, "You already have, Luke, you were right about me. Tell your sister [Leia] you were right."

One

The number of outfits Han Solo wears throughout the original trilogy.

Most of the Tatooine-set scenes for *Star Wars Episode IV: A New Hope* were filmed in the Tunisian desert, where the rough conditions led to all kinds of mechanical malfunctions with R2-D2 and other machines. The crew was also working with a limited budget. Key scenes, like when the Jawas capture R2-D2 early in the film, had to be filmed in Death Valley, California.

⊰1971⊱

The year Lucasfilm was created, initially to protect George Lucas from personal lawsuits.

If you're waiting for a remastered original trilogy on DVD or Blu-ray without Lucas' later edits or the new footage he shot years after the fact, don't hold your breath. The website *OriginalTrilogy.com* created a petition for Lucasfilm to release what could be called an unspecial Special Edition—one without the additional CGI, the ghost of Anakin Skywalker at the end of the series, and so on. The response was immediate: 10,000 online signatures in the first 24 hours and nearly 80,000 within a couple of months. According to the website, Lucasfilm's public relations department responded with a strongly worded rejection letter that implied the original *Star Wars* trilogy negatives were gone.

Despite coming two decades after the original trilogy, episodes I through III were already outlined long before shooting began. Lucas wrote the backstory for every character featured in *Episode IV: A New Hope*, perhaps inspired by J. R. R. Tolkien's belief that creating a believable universe requires knowing more about it than you share with the audience. Lucas wasn't sure he'd have the opportunity to tell the previous stories, but once the original trilogy was done, he fleshed out what he'd written years before.

Revisiting the first three episodes created some retroactive changes too. For example, the concept of midichlorians, the blood-borne bacteria behind the Force, wasn't mentioned at all in the first trilogy. Of course, it also led to cosmetic changes in later versions of the first trilogy, like Anakin's ghost being added to the final scene of *Star Wars VI: The Return of the Jedi*.

QUESTION:

What is Order 66?

   a. Eliminate all the living Jedis

   b. Destroy the Death Star

   c. Freeze Han Solo

   d. Eat the Ewoks

ANSWER:

a. Eliminate all the living Jedis

Science fiction was a financially unproven genre in the 1970s, so 20th Century Fox balked when Lucas requested $13 million to make *Star Wars Episode IV: A New Hope*. In fact, the studio insisted that the budget had to be under $10 million, which was sizable at the time. Lucas asked for $9,999,000.99. He ended up spending about $13 million of 20th Century Fox's money.

It worked out all right for 20th Century Fox. By the time the film finished its run, the studio's $13 million investment had raked in about $750 million in theaters worldwide.

The name of the cuddly Ewoks was inspired by a real-life Native America tribe, the Miwok. Lucas didn't have to go far for inspiration, as the Miwok's native land is now part of the Redwood National Park. This Northern California forest is close to where Lucas eventually set up Skywalker Ranch, and it is also where he filmed the Ewok scenes in *Star Wars VI: The Return of the Jedi*.

QUESTION:

Which of these actors was reportedly seriously considered for the role of Han Solo?

a. Mark Hamill

b. Billy Dee Williams

c. Al Pacino

d. Robin Williams

ANSWER:

c. Al Pacino

Nick Nolte, Christopher Walken, and Kurt Russell were also rumored to be in the running. Pacino was already working with Lucas' friend and mentor, Francis Ford Coppola, on the successful Godfather series.

Mark Hamill was in a severe car accident right before he finished filming *Star Wars Episode IV: A New Hope*. He fractured his left cheekbone and nose. A double was used in the final scenes. In *Star Wars Episode V: The Empire Strikes Back*, Hamill's more rugged look matched the storyline's older, war-seasoned Luke Skywalker.

Next to *The Phantom Menace, Star Wars Episode VI: The Return of the Jedi* was easily the most anticipated movie in the entire series. Paranoid about people snooping around while they were filming, George Lucas gave the movie a code name: "Blue Harvest." He even made a logo and had the film crew wear Blue Harvest gear. It later became the name of Seth MacFarlane's popular Star Wars satire-homage, *Family Guy: Blue Harvest*, which featured tongue-in-cheek voice work from actors like Chevy Chase, Adam West, and even Rush Limbaugh playing himself.

QUESTION:

What is the name of Chewbacca's planet?

  a. Kashyyyk

  b. Tatooine

  c. Deep Space 9

  d. Vulcan

ANSWER:

a. Kashyyyk

It also goes by the scientific name
G5-623. There isn't a common Earth
language that has any words with
three Ys in a row.

The first *Star Wars* movie was not an easy experience for C-3PO actor Anthony Daniels. The mechanical costume was stiff, confining, and noisy. The biggest problem, though, was the heat. It was remarkably hot while they were filming in North Africa, with Tunisian desert temperatures regularly well over 100 degrees Fahrenheit, and Daniels passed out several times. The crew eventually figured out how to push cool air into his heavy suit, which prevented him from overheating as quickly.

The C-3PO costume was also so noisy that it muffled Daniels' voice, as well as everyone else's dialogue. Daniels and any surrounding actors had to perform their scenes first and re-record their lines in the studio. It's possible that this is why C-3PO waves his arms around so much; Daniels may have been trying to communicate in any way possible.

The largest known collection of Star Wars memorabilia can be found at Rancho Obi-Wan. A nonprofit run by former Lucasfilm Head of Fan Relations Sam Sansweet, Rancho Obi-Wan has more than 300,000 Star Wars–related pieces in a 9,000-square-foot space that formerly housed a hatchery for 20,000 chickens. Sansweet's accumulation began three decades ago in his greater Los Angeles home but eventually migrated to Petaluma, California, near Skywalker Ranch. Plan your trip now: It's open to the public.

QUESTION:

After wrapping up the first *Star Wars* trilogy, Mark Hamill moved to voice acting. Which of the following *hasn't* Hamill contributed his voice to?

a. *Batman: The Animated Series*

b. *The Simpsons*

c. *Wing Commander*

d. *Grand Theft Auto: Vice City*

ANSWER:

d. *Grand Theft Auto: Vice City*

Mark Hamill has also continued to act in the occasional live-action film. One of his more notable cameos was playing a villain in Kevin Smith's 2001 comedy *Jay and Silent Bob Strike Back* (which also featured a cameo by Carrie Fisher as a nun). In a lightsaber duel, Hamill's character's hand is lopped off, leaving him to look at the camera and groan, "Not again."

TRUE OR FALSE?

In *Star Wars Episode III: Revenge of the Sith*, every clone trooper onscreen is computer-generated.

TRUE.

Composed of more than 2,000 computer-generated shots, the special effects took two years to create.

Star Wars set props (everything from pieces of the Death Star model to Darth Vader's helmet) always sell for big bucks, but the most expensive sold thus far is a Panavision PSR R-200 camera. The 35mm device, which Lucas used for principal photography on *Star Wars Episode IV: A New Hope*, went for $625,000 in a 2011 auction.

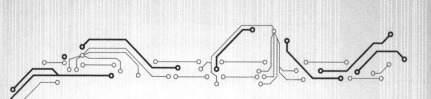

QUESTION:

Who began the project that would become the Death Star?

- a. **Palpatine**
- b. **Boba Fett**
- c. **Count Dooku**
- d. **Lando Calrissian**

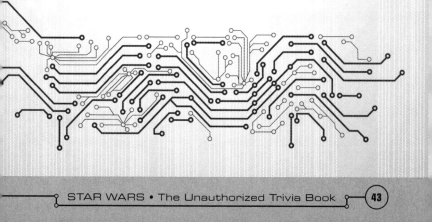

ANSWER:

a. Palpatine

Darth Sidious began construction of the Death Star, nicknamed "The Ultimate Weapon," right after forming the Galactic Empire.

QUESTION:

Who else was up for Carrie Fisher's Princess Leia role?

QUESTION:

Chronologically, when did moviegoers first see under Darth Vader's mask?

ANSWER:

Amy Irving, Sissy Spacek, and Jodie Foster

Irving was an actor and Steven Spielberg's one-time wife, Spacek hit stardom with the 1976 horror film *Carrie*, and Foster would later become an Academy Award–winning actor and director.

ANSWER:

Star Wars V: The Empire Strikes Back

The scene occurs nearly an hour into the movie, when Vader puts on his helmet. We see only the back of his head, which is hairless and looks somewhat sickly.

QUESTION:

According to Star Wars lore, what are the Three Pillars of the Jedi?

ANSWER:

The Force—Consistently reaching a heightened mental state similar to meditation and (based on the second trilogy) a heightened physical state from blood-borne bacteria called midichlorians.

Knowledge—Understanding Jedi history, based on in-depth study of the archives in the gigantic library at the Jedi Temple on the planet of Coruscant.

Self-discipline—Building the focus necessary to center oneself and, eventually, master the lightsaber.

Every year, the Library of Congress selects 25 films to be added to the prestigious National Film Registry, its collection of "culturally, historically or aesthetically" significant works of cinema. George Lucas has four films in the National Film Registry. They are:

- 1967's *THX 1138* (added in 2010)

- 1973's *American Graffiti* (added in 1995)

- 1977's *Star Wars Episode IV: A New Hope* (added in 1989)

- 1980's *Star Wars Episode V: The Empire Strikes Back* (added in 2010)

Almost
1
percent

The amount of UK residents who declared their religion as "Jedi" on the 2001 census.

One of the earliest examples of computer-generated graphics onscreen appears in the first *Star Wars*. The Death Star briefing sequence for the Rebel pilots shows computerized, line-based visuals on the monitors. Until then, visuals were usually done with stop-motion animation or cell-based drawings. Computer-based graphics would significantly save time: Stop-motion animation required moving an object a fraction of an inch, filming it, and moving it again, while cell-based animation required hand-drawing each frame of the scene.

The first Star Wars arcade game, named simply Star Wars Arcade, used the same line-based animation technique in 1983. By then, the newest *Star Wars*, *The Return of the Jedi*, used much more advanced computer-aided graphics.

Star Wars Episode IV: A New Hope originally had three different sound mixes. The first two released were a two-channel Dolby stereo mix for the 35mm version of the movie and a six-track stereo mix for the 70mm version. Later in 1977, the studio released a monaural mix for single-speaker movie theaters.

The *Star Wars* saga's biggest inspiration came from classic serials like *Flash Gordon* and *Buck Rogers*. Popular in 1930s theaters, serials left audiences with weekly cliffhangers. Television drastically changed the movie serial formula, moving the weekly concept to TV, while theatrical films were almost entirely stand-alone entities.

It's probably not a coincidence that the very same serials that inspired Lucas were resurrected after the success of *Star Wars*. *Buck Rogers in the 25th Century* (a science-

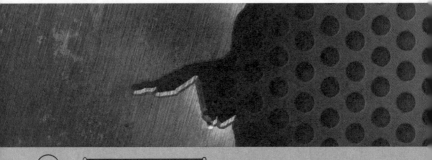

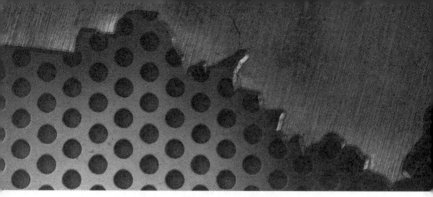

fiction novel first adapted as a film serial in 1939) was a hit TV show on NBC from 1979 to 1981, starring Gil Gerard as the hero as well as Erin Gray, later of *Silver Spoons* fame.

The feature film of *Flash Gordon* (based on the popular comic strip and numerous film serials that began in 1936) finally hit theaters in 1980, with a cast that included future James Bond portrayer Timothy Dalton, *Fiddler on the Roof* star Topol, *The Rocky Horror Picture Show*'s Richard O'Brien, and classic actor Max von Sydow as Emperor Ming the Merciless.

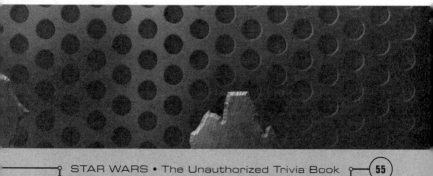

DAMON BROWN

10 HOURS

The amount of time it took to create the illusion of Yoda using the Force to lift Luke's X-Wing out of the Dagobah swamp in *Star Wars Episode V: The Empire Strikes Back*.

1,000,000

The number of copies the official *Star Wars* soundtrack sold in the first year.

The famous Princess Leia hologram scene from *Star Wars Episode IV: A New Hope*, in which she implores the long-reclusive Obi-Wan Kenobi for help in battling the Empire, took three days to film. The team recorded Carrie Fisher from multiple camera angles, then filtered the footage through a television. They then shot a flashlight over the image, making the resulting flickering image look like it was being beamed from R2-D2.

It would have been recorded faster, but Lucas couldn't decide if Leia looked better with her hood up or down, so they filmed both.

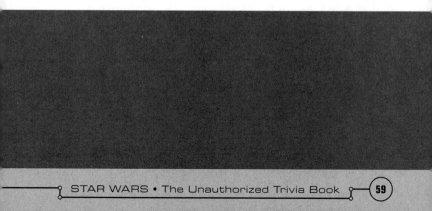

n *Star Wars Episode V: The Empire Strikes Back*, Han Solo keeps a wounded Luke Skywalker from freezing by using Luke's lightsaber to slice open the belly of the dead Tauntaun (the furry creatures that Rebel soldiers rode like horses on the ice planet Hoth) and putting him inside the warm body. This survival method isn't original. Lucas learned about it from Native Americans and Eskimos who, in worst-case scenarios, hid within their animal prey to stay warm.

In 1977, *Star Wars* didn't just look original—it *sounded* unique too. Lucas didn't want the then-standard space-age bleeps and bloops. Instead, he insisted on realistic sounds. For example, his sound-design team recorded real-world jet-engine noises to echo through the starships. Most of the audio footage was then played and re-recorded in echo-heavy areas like bathrooms to convey sound in space.

The Academy of Motion Picture Arts and Sciences recognized the original *Star Wars* with an Oscar for Best Sound (Mixing) and another for the sequel *Star Wars Episode V: The Empire Strikes Back*. It nominated both *Star Wars Episode VI: The Return of the Jedi* and *Star Wars Episode I: The Phantom Menace* for Best Sound Editing and Best Sound (Mixing).

The Star Wars series has filmed all around the globe, including in these countries:

- Australia
- Tunisia
- Spain
- Norway
- Italy

To put it mildly, Lucas has gotten some heat for making changes in the 1997 *Star Wars IV–VI* "Special Edition" theatrical re-releases, but few were as controversial as Greedo shooting first. In the original *Star Wars IV: A New Hope*, Han Solo ruthlessly blasts space hunter Greedo in a bar. In the revamp, Greedo shoots and misses before Han Solo pops the alien, turning it from a shrewd if cold-blooded move to an act of justifiable self-defense. Fans were outraged.

From that point on, "Greedo Shoots First" became popular shorthand for any ill-conceived idea. Fans would later use the term to describe midichlorians, the controversial bacteria used to scientifically explain the Force, as well as the generally loathed character Jar Jar Binks.

QUESTION:

In *Star Wars*, Greedo the Bounty Hunter's language is based on a real-life dialect from where?

    a. Taiwan

    b. Peru

    c. Alaska

    d. Kenya

ANSWER:

b. Peru

Lucas' special dialogue and sound-effects guy, Ben Burtt (who later worked on all manner of science-fiction films, from *E.T.* to *WALL-E*), created Greedo's unique vocal patterns by hiring a linguistics student to record the dialogue in the ancient Incan dialect of Quechua and then electronically distorting the results.

1982

The year the first Star Wars game was released: Parker Brothers' Star Wars: The Empire Strikes Back for the Atari 2600. In the game, players fly small landspeeders over the surface of the planet Hoth as they try and destroy Imperial AT-AT Walkers before they can reach the Rebel base.

$100,000,000

The amount the original *Star Wars* earned in its first three months of release.

Darth Vader may be the easiest Star Wars character to impersonate next to Jar Jar Binks, but his signature heavy breathing was a much more complex creation. Vader's voice originally had a lot of computerized sounds, but they were loud and made it difficult to hear dialogue during his scenes. The sound team settled on Vader sounding like he had a breathing apparatus. To make the sound, they used an actual self-contained underwater breathing apparatus—SCUBA gear.

QUESTION:

James Earl Jones gave Darth Vader his famously deep voice, but who actually played Darth Vader?

QUESTION:

How does Princess Leia respond to Han Solo's declaration of "I love you" in *Star Wars Episode VI: The Return of the Jedi*?

ANSWER:

David Prowse

Prowse, a former English body builder, wasn't confident that *Star Wars* was going to be a success. In fact, he reportedly was so sure it was going to fail, he asked that his name be removed from the original movie credits. He changed his mind later.

ANSWER:

"I know."

It is the counterpoint to when Princess Leia declares her love for Han Solo in *Star Wars Episode V: The Empire Strikes Back*, just before he is frozen in carbonite.

The light from the lightsaber initially wasn't bright enough, so the team drew a highlighted, animated effect during the editing process. It was done old school, with an animator creating the lightsaber light on each frame of the scenes.

Technology advanced considerably after *Star Wars Episode IV: A New Hope*, so later movies didn't have to rely on the cell-based animation.

Lucas sanctioned official radio adaptations of the first three *Star Wars* films, which were produced by National Public Radio and broadcast in 1981 (*A New Hope*), 1983 (*The Empire Strikes Back*), and 1996 (*The Return of the Jedi*). Mark Hamill, Billy Dee Williams, and other stars from the original movies returned to do the voice acting.

TRUE OR FALSE?

Leonardo DiCaprio was considered for the role of Anakin Skywalker in the second trilogy.

TRUE.

Ryan Phillippe and Colin Hanks (Tom Hanks' son) were also up for the part.

Star Wars has spawned dozens of novels, but the first book came out before *A New Hope* even hit theaters. Arriving on November 12, 1976, *Star Wars: From the Adventures of Luke Skywalker* was an adaptation of the upcoming film. Although sci-fi novelist Alan Dean Foster ghostwrote the book, George Lucas was listed as its author. Foster also wrote 1978's *Splinter of the Mind's Eye*, the first novel based on Star Wars characters that contained events not depicted in the films.

A shrewd businessman, George Lucas demanded the profits from the first *Star Wars* movie soundtrack as well as any related merchandise. 20th Century Fox didn't think much of this request, given that at the time soundtracks rarely made money and ancillary products brought in even less. John Williams' *Star Wars* theme ended up being one of the most covered songs of the 1970s and, of course, Star Wars posters, toys, and video games helped make Lucas a billionaire. Star Wars products alone bring in more than $1 billion annually.

T o keep things as realistic as possible, sets for the first trilogy of *Star Wars* films were made to look thoroughly lived-in. Although the films were science fiction, Lucas wanted them to have as much verisimilitude as possible. Metal panels were scuffed, walls were scratched, and other details were purposely distressed. Lucas wanted the *Millennium Falcon* and all the vehicles to look like they had been through war.

$4,050,000,000

The amount of money The Walt Disney Company paid for Lucasfilm in May 2012. The same year, Lucas made the *Forbes* magazine list of the world's richest billionaires, with an estimated total worth of $3.9 billion, just ahead of his friend Steven Spielberg ($3.2 billion).

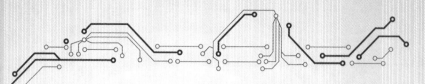

QUESTION:

Which *Star Wars* film earned the Golden Raspberry award for Worst Screenplay?

a. *Star Wars Episode II: Attack of the Clones*

b. *Star Wars Episode III: Revenge of the Sith*

c. *Star Wars Episode V: The Empire Strikes Back*

d. *Star Wars Episode I: The Phantom Menace*

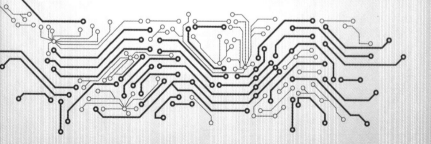

ANSWER:

a. *Star Wars Episode II: Attack of the Clones*

The first *Star Wars* trilogy did incredibly well in the box office, especially considering that the movies' production costs were low compared to the later trilogy (the numbers below don't include the millions also generated by DVD, VHS, and Blu-ray sales):

- *A New Hope* cost $13 million, earned $775 million

- *The Empire Strikes Back* cost $32 million, earned $538 million

- *The Return of the Jedi* cost $32.5 million, earned $475 million

Every *Star Wars* film took less than a year to film (although post-production and special-effects work were a different story):

- *Star Wars Episode IV: A New Hope*: several months in 1977

- *Star Wars Episode V: The Empire Strikes Back*: March–September 1980

- *Star Wars Episode VI: The Return of the Jedi*: January–May 1982

- *Star Wars Episode I: The Phantom Menace*: June–December 1997

- *Star Wars Episode II: Attack of the Clones*: June–September 2000

- *Star Wars Episode III: Revenge of the Sith*: three secret months in 2003

Conceived as eco-friendly before it was trendy, the Star Wars universe uses little to no paper. The civilizations are apparently so advanced that all information is saved in a digital form, hence we never see paper throughout the entire series. Evidently the Empire is intent on ruling the universe, but also cares about the environment.

⋘ **Four** ⋙

The number of full screenplay drafts of *Star Wars Episode IV: A New Hope* George Lucas wrote before he said he got it right. Legend has it that a thoroughly unimpressed Harrison Ford griped to Lucas while they were filming, "You can write this s***, George, but you can't say it."

QUESTION:

How did the crew make the sound of Darth Vader crushing someone's neck?

a. Crushing walnut shells on top of a grapefruit

b. Crushing M&Ms underneath a thick-heeled boot

c. Crushing ice on a metal surface

d. Crushing chicken bones on a Brillo pad

ANSWER:

a. Crushing walnut shells on top of a grapefruit

Lucas made a conscious choice for almost every aesthetic decision throughout the series. The best example is the color schemes. The Empire is always represented in black and white, showing its commitment to military discipline and its extreme ideals. Lucas calls the Empire universe "a world of absolutes." On the other hand, non-Empire worlds are represented by earthy hues like green, blue, and brown.

George Lucas' first film, *THX 1138*, bombed so badly at the box office that Warner Bros. took back its multifilm deal with Lucas and his mentor, Francis Ford Coppola, thereby losing the opportunity to release future classics like *Apocalypse Now*—and, of course, *Star Wars*.

Boba Fett dies a simple death in *Star Wars VI: The Return of the Jedi* (he is swallowed by a sandworm), but Lucas says it would have been much more dramatic if he had known how popular the character would be with future fans. He contemplated adding more footage to the 1997 Special Editions, but ultimately decided against it—potentially avoiding a "Greedo Shoots First"-esque fan fit.

$20,000

The amount United Artists paid George Lucas for doing *American Graffiti*. The film left him $15,000 in debt before it became a hit.

Right before filming *Star Wars*, Lucas bought a large, secluded Victorian home in San Anselmo, California, that was large enough to house his collaborators. When new neighbors purchased nearby land and started building houses, Lucas swept in and bought those properties. He wanted privacy. His complex of buildings marked the start of what would become Skywalker Ranch.

Skywalker Ranch has livestock and gardens, as well as a man-made pond called Lake Ewok. Today it reportedly takes up 4,700 acres, but few people know the actual size—it isn't open to the public.

Additions included in the 1997 *Star Wars* trilogy Special Edition theatrical re-release:

- Anakin Skywalker's spirit appears alongside Obi-Wan Kenobi and Yoda at the end of *Star Wars VI: The Return of the Jedi*

- A CGI scene where Jabba the Hutt and Han Solo talk before Luke and Obi-Wan aboard the Millennium Falcon is inserted into *Star Wars Episode IV: A New Hope*

- Greedo shoots first in the cantina scene in *Episode IV*

- James Earl Jones is credited for the voice of Darth Vader

- Subtitles are added to Jabba the Hutt's dialogue in *Episode VI*

QUESTION:

Sir Christopher Lee played the evil Count Dooku in the *Star Wars* films, but he also played a villain in which of these films?

a. *Evil Dead 2*

b. *Gremlins*

c. *The Lord of the Rings: The Fellowship of the Ring*

d. *Harry Potter and the Order of the Phoenix*

ANSWER:

c. *The Lord of the Rings: The Fellowship of the Ring*

ndustrial Light and Magic opened in June 1975 specifically to handle the state-of-the-art effects for *Star Wars Episode IV: A New Hope*. The first special effect good enough to make it into the final movie wasn't created until October 1976. It was the Death Star shooting a laser.

The scene in *Star Wars Episode V: The Empire Strikes Back* when the heroes accidently land the *Millennium Falcon* inside of a giant worm was created the old-fashioned way, even by 1980s standards. The deadly flying birds were plastic puppets hanging on fishing poles. The worm that swallowed the heroes was actually a hand puppet that was only a few inches big.

DAMON BROWN

QUESTION:

Which *Star Wars* film is the longest?

a. *Star Wars Episode I:
   The Phantom Menace*

b. *Star Wars Episode V:
   The Empire Strikes Back*

c. *Star Wars Episode II:
   Attack of the Clones*

d. *Star Wars Episode IV:
   A New Hope*

ANSWER:

c. *Star Wars Episode II: Attack of the Clones* (142 minutes)

George Lucas was a recent, unemployed graduate just a few years before he filmed *Star Wars*. In fact, he was so desperate to get a job, he applied to the Air Force during the Vietnam War because he thought he could be hired as an armed forces photographer. The Air Force rejected him because he got too many speeding tickets as a teenager. His fast-paced, hot-rod adolescence ended up being the inspiration for his first hit, 1973's semi-autobiographical *American Graffiti*.

Obi-Wan Kenobi was originally going to teach Luke Skywalker how to use the Force effectively in *Star Wars Episode V: The Empire Strikes Back*. However, when the precursor, *Star Wars Episode IV: A New Hope*, was filmed, Lucas and his team decided to kill Obi-Wan, thereby making it impossible for him to teach Luke in the next movie. Lucas realized he needed to create another powerful Jedi: Yoda.

Yoda was a two-foot puppet designed by Jim Henson and his team, the folks behind The Muppets and 1980s fantasy movies like *Labyrinth* and *The Dark Crystal*. Yoda's face, developed by the late Stuart Freeborn, was reportedly modeled after *The Empire Strikes Back* director Irvin Kershner.

QUESTION:

Which comedian was *not* a guest star in the 1978 *Star Wars Holiday Special*?

    a. Art Carney
    b. Harvey Korman
    c. Bea Arthur
    d. Carol Burnett

ANSWER:

d. Carol Burnett

Also on the truly strange list of performers who appeared in this infamous and (since then) little-seen special were the band Jefferson Starship and actress Diahann Carroll (as a holograph).

The giant *Millennium Falcon* ship model in *Star Wars Episode V: The Empire Strikes Back* could barely move, so director Irvin Kershner tilted the camera during the wild dogfight scenes. He told Ford, Fisher, and the other actors when to throw themselves the appropriate way.

In an attempt to connect with citizens, the Barack Obama administration announced that it would consider any petition signed by more than 10,000 U.S. residents. In 2012, nearly 35,000 Americans made their interest very clear on the White House website: Secure resources and funding, and begin construction of a Death Star by 2016. The petition argued that "[b]y focusing our defense resources into a space-superiority platform and weapon system such as a Death Star, the government can spur job creation in the fields of construction, engineering, space exploration, and more, and strengthen our national defense."

The White House, by its own rules, was required to respond.

In a blog post titled "This Isn't the Petition Response You're Looking For," the White House provided several reasons why it would not begin construction of a Death Star, including the fact that the Death Star has been estimated "to cost more than $850,000,000,000,000,000" and "the Administration does not support blowing up planets."

Star Wars Episode IV: A New Hope uses rapidly edited scenes during its fighting sequences to emulate documentary footage from World Wars I and II. (Supposedly early test screenings of the film were shown before the special effects were completed, and Lucas substituted dogfight footage for the climactic X-Wing and Tie-Fighter battle around the Death Star.) The sudden movements make the battles feel more intense, particularly the final fight with the Death Star. The creators also admitted that quick cuts helped hide any flaws in their low-resolution shots!

In *Star Wars Episode V: The Empire Strikes Back*, Yoda was essentially a hand puppet with several engineers manipulating its eyes, ears, and other parts via remote control. The team hid underneath the camera shots and used several monitors below to see what was happening onscreen as they worked. The only puppet more elaborate than Yoda was Jabba the Hutt, which required up to 10 different operators, mostly for its face.

TRUE OR FALSE?

American Graffiti took George Lucas longer to film than each of the movies in the first *Star Wars* trilogy.

TRUE.

Incredibly, although they were exponentially more complicated from a technical standpoint, the first *Star Wars* trilogy films took a year or less each to direct. *American Graffiti*, whose most complicated shots involved a couple of racing hot rods, took two years.

Lando Calrissian actor Billy Dee Williams was one of the few household names cast in the first *Star Wars* trilogy. By 1977, he had already starred in box-office hits like the football drama *Brian's Song* and two Diana Ross vehicles, *Lady Sings the Blues* and *Mahogany*. George Lucas took a serious risk in keeping Calrissian's role to a minimum in the second *Star Wars* film after killing off the young series' only other character played by a well-known actor, Sir Alec Guinness' Obi-Wan Kenobi.

Darth Vader's echoing, ominous footsteps were recorded in a series of secret underground military tunnels underneath the Marin Headlands, a landmark near San Francisco's Golden Gate Bridge. The area was gated off from the public, but the sound team snuck through a loose set of bars and recorded someone walking down the long halls in heavy boots.

The speedsters in *Star Wars Episode VI: The Return of the Jedi* were taller than the actual Ewoks. The Ewok actors were around two feet tall, while the speedsters were approximately three feet off the ground. In a few key shots, like when an Ewok steals a speedster, the crew threw the actor from offscreen onto the bike!

⋙ 3 feet ⋘

The actual size of the Death Star
model in the original *Star Wars*.
The model for the *Millennium Falcon*
measured just four feet. In 2012,
students at Lehigh University
attempted to calculate the actual
size of a real-life Death Star. They
determined that it was 140 kilometers
(about 87 miles) wide and would have
required more than one *quadrillion* tons
of steel to construct.

15

The original *Star Wars* ranking among the American Film Institute's 100 best movies of all time. The top three were *Citizen Kane*, *Casablanca*, and *The Godfather*, the last of which was directed by Lucas' mentor, Francis Ford Coppola. Lucas' *American Graffiti* came in at 77.

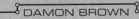

Conductor John Williams is as much a part of the success of *Star Wars* as the main actors or even Lucas himself. Beginning with his Oscar nomination for 1967's *Valley of the Dolls*, Williams became recognized for bringing intense, emotional classical scores to film. A decade later, he won Original Best Score for the first *Star Wars* and was later nominated for *Episode V: The Empire Strikes Back* and *Episode VI: The Return of the Jedi*.

Williams' original *Star Wars* theme in particular has stood the test of time, as the song is immediately clear from its opening crescendo. *Episode IV: A New Hope* was his third Oscar win after 1971's *Fiddler on the Roof*, based on the classic Broadway musical, and 1975's *Jaws*, which was directed by Lucas' colleague, Steven Spielberg. Williams went on to score many other films for both Spielberg and Lucas, including the second *Star Wars* trilogy.

Majestic music is a hallmark of *Episodes IV and V*, except for one particular set of scenes: lightsaber battles. Sound engineer Ben Burtt purposely left any lightsaber scene free of music so the audience would be fully focused on the steady hum and electric clash of the swords. He felt the sound effects were their own kind of music.

While filming *Star Wars Episode IV: A New Hope* in Tunisia, a heavy sandstorm wrecked the Tatooine backdrop and halted filming for days. Two decades later, when Lucas filmed *Star Wars Episode I: The Phantom Menace*, the same thing happened to the new Tatooine backdrop. Lucas reportedly considered this a good omen for the second trilogy.

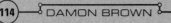

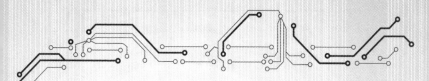

QUESTION:

Princess Leia disguised her voice when she snuck in to save Han Solo from Jabba the Hutt's lair. Pat Walsh did the voice-over for Carrie Fisher—and also the voice for what other 1980s hit science-fiction film?

- a. *The Terminator*
- b. *E.T.: The Extra-Terrestrial*
- c. *Robocop*
- d. *Tron*

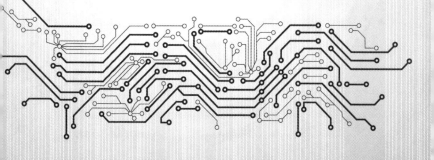

ANSWER:

b. *E.T.: The Extra-Terrestrial*

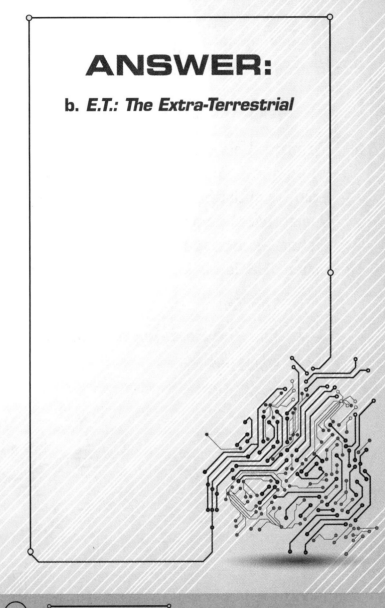

DAMON BROWN

The Empire's clothing changes from normal garments in episodes I through III to tight, restricted uniforms in episodes IV through VI. The later military garb represents how the Empire, not the Jedis, have become the power within the Star Wars universe. Lucas said the biggest inspiration for the Empire's military uniforms were those worn by the Nazis.

Some sounds that were used throughout the Star Wars series were indirectly from Ken Strickfaden, a legendary sounds engineer best known for the 1931 film *Frankenstein*. *Star Wars* sound engineer Ben Burtt visited Strickfaden before his death and recorded the sounds generated by some of the odd electrical equipment Strickfaden still had in his studio.

Jabba the Hutt isn't a CGI creation, but a really big puppet. It was controlled by a little person in the tail and several people inside and beneath the body manipulating the eyes, tongue, and facial features. The puppet was so complicated that the floor of the set was raised four feet off the stage floor to accommodate all the puppeteers.

In the original manuscript, the *Star Wars Episode VI: The Return of the Jedi* plot was only about 20 pages—far too short for a feature-length film. Many scenes, including the lengthy storyline with Jabba the Hutt, weren't included. The problem stemmed from the way the piece was originally written: What ended up becoming episodes IV, V, and VI was originally conceived as one epic, 200-minute movie. Once Lucas began filming *The Return of the Jedi*, he realized he needed to expand the story.

By Lucas' own admission, he didn't really think about how the story would break into a proper trilogy until late in the process. As he began to flesh out the individual films, he realized what parts were longer, like *A New Hope*, and what parts were significantly shorter. It's important to note that plot twists considered significant now, like Obi-Wan Kenobi returning to the Force at the end of *A New Hope* or Han Solo surviving in the carbonite for *The Return of the Jedi*, weren't settled until right before filming or, in some cases, during filming.

The Han Solo carbonite-freezing scene in *Star Wars Episode V: The Empire Strikes Back* differed in two ways from Lucas' original intentions. First, when Leia says "I love you," Han was going to say "I love you too," but director Irvin Kershner didn't think the response fit his character—he might love her, but he wouldn't be that soft. The cast brainstormed for an hour and, on the last take before giving up, Ford uttered the "I know" line. Second, the carbonite casing initially had Han Solo's frame with arms at his side, as if he was in a casket. Kershner argued that Han wouldn't be at peace with being frozen into a slab. Instead, he'd be in a fighting, agonized stance, which is what the final cut showed.

QUESTION:

Warwick Davis' strong turn as the Ewok Wicket in *Star Wars Episode VI: The Return of the Jedi* led to him starring in what 1988 movie?

a. *Who Framed Roger Rabbit?*

b. *Big*

c. *Beetlejuice*

d. *Willow*

d. *Willow*

This 1988 fantasy epic about a dwarf
who must protect a baby girl from a
sorceress queen was directed by Ron
Howard from a story idea by Lucas,
who executive produced.

The original *Star Wars* was carried by a surprisingly young cast. Mark Hamill was in his early twenties during filming, while Harrison Ford (in his early thirties), was considered the elder statesman. In his sixties, Sir Alec Guinness was likely the oldest actor on the set. By May 1977, Carrie Fisher was five months away from her twenty-first birthday—too young to drink legally at the film's premiere.

A man of habit, George Lucas wrote *American Graffiti*, *Star Wars Episode IV: A New Hope*, and *Star Wars Episode I: The Phantom Menace* on the same binder of yellow paper. Word has it he always demands the same blue-and-green-lined paper and a special kind of number 2 pencil.

The whole thing about Darth Vader being Luke's father? It was George Lucas' and director Irvin Kershner's secret until the audiences saw *Star Wars Episode V: The Empire Strikes Back* in theaters. According to Lucas, he didn't tell the actors—he didn't even tell Kershner until the last moment. He was afraid the knowledge would taint the acting and direction of the movie. Darth Vader's lips are hidden throughout the film, so they were able to overdub the "Luke, I am your father" line into the film's final cut. Hamill's terror is a reaction to Vader cutting his hand off, not the paternity news. In the end, the actors were as shocked as the audience itself.

QUESTION:

C-3PO's design was inspired by what classic robot movie?

a. *Forbidden Planet*

b. *Hugo*

c. *The Day The Earth Stood Still*

d. *Metropolis*

ANSWER:

d. Metropolis

In Fritz Lang's 1927 science-fiction classic, one of the central figures is a sleek and beautiful female-looking robot, one of the first ever to appear on screen.

The respected publisher Dark Horse Comics has issued almost 100 different Star Wars series or stand-alone comics, an impressive number considering it started producing the books only two decades ago. Dark Horse's first Star Wars work was 1991's *Dark Empire*, a six-issue series lasting from winter 1991 to fall 1992. Unlike the first Star Wars comics from Marvel, the Dark Horse comics had a heavier, more adult style. And in a departure from the long-running Marvel series, *Dark Empire* took place after the movies ended—specifically, after Darth Vader's death.

Infamous bounty hunter Boba Fett was inspired by the "man with no name" from Sergio Leone's classic spaghetti westerns. Like the nameless antihero from *A Fistful of Dollars* or *The Good, The Bad, and The Ugly*, Boba Fett is a mysterious, violent character who we find ourselves silently rooting for. Fett is one of the most popular action figures sold, and he also inspired several bands, including the punk outfit Boba Fett Youth.

The fearsome, rancorous beast in Jabba the Hutt's basement dungeon who nearly eats Luke Skywalker before he can rescue Han Solo is made up of two things: an arm and a dog. The massive-looking puppet was a 16-inch design that fit snugly on the puppeteer's arm. The growl came from a small dachshund in the sound engineer's neighborhood.

*S*tar Wars Episode II: Attack of the Clones was the only film of the two trilogies that did not top the box office the year it came out. *Spider-Man*, *The Lord of the Rings: The Two Towers*, and *Harry Potter and the Chamber of Secrets* all outshone *Clones* in ticket sales for 2002.

*W*hen Lando Calrissian manned the *Millennium Falcon* in *Star Wars VI: The Return of the Jedi*, his co-pilot was the Sullustan alien Nien Nunb. The seemingly alien speech is actually a Kenyan dialect. Voice actor Kipsang Rotich used accurate language, enough so audience members understood what Nien Nunb was saying when the movie premiered in Kenya.

QUESTION:

What item was *not* used to make the sound of AT-AT Walkers moving in *Star Wars Episode V: The Empire Strikes Back* and *Star Wars VI: The Return of the Jedi*?

- a. A metal-shearing machine
- b. A screaming child
- c. A dumpster lid
- d. An explosion in a field

ANSWER:

b. A screaming child

The *Star Wars* movies are among the biggest blockbusters of all time. Here is how they rank in terms of total box-office revenue:

- *Star Wars Episode I: The Phantom Menace*: 11

- *Star Wars Episode II: Attack of the Clones*: 61

- *Star Wars Episode III: Revenge of the Sith*: 30

- *Star Wars Episode IV: A New Hope*: 41

- *Star Wars Episode V: The Empire Strikes Back*: 92

- *Star Wars Episode VI: The Return of the Jedi*: 117

The fan website *StarWarsUncut.com* sliced *A New Hope* into hundreds of key scenes and asked visitors to film their own renditions of favorite scenes. Fans represented all 400 clips within three days, with interpretations as varied as stick drawings, stop-action LEGOs, and live-action cats.

THE RANKS OF JEDI:

- **Jedi Initiate**: A youngling born with the Force in his or her blood

- **Jedi Padawan**: An adolescent or young adult who has completed early Jedi tests called The Initiate Trials and is under Jedi Master tutelage

- **Jedi Knight**: A Padawan who successfully received a decade of one-on-one training with a Jedi Master

- **Jedi Master**: A Knight who has successfully completed the Jedi Trials and trained at least one Padawan to Knight status

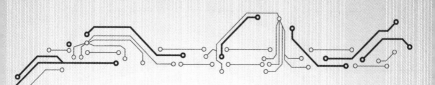

QUESTION:

What does the word "Yoda" mean in Sanskrit?

QUESTION:

What was the name of the first *Star Wars* synopsis?

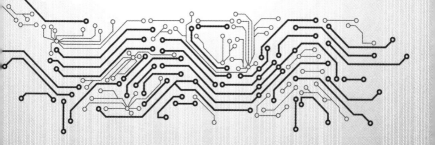

ANSWER:

Warrior

It is traditionally spelled
"Yoddha."

ANSWER:

*The Journey of
the Whills*

It was a two-page description
that bears little resemblance
to the final screenplay.

The first Star Wars comic was published on April 12, 1977, about a month before the original film hit theaters. Loosely based on the beginning of *A New Hope*, *Star Wars 1* has the Empire capturing Princess Leia while two droids, R2-D2 and C-3PO, manage to escape. The duo eventually connect with Luke Skywalker, but R2-D2 leaves the Skywalker farm in search of Obi-Wan Kenobi, who it believes can save Princess Leia. Marvel Comics published 107 issues in the first Star Wars series through 1986.

George Lucas wasn't always driven. In fact, he never did well in school and didn't have much ambition. He might have become an underachiever if he hadn't been in a serious car accident as a teenager. Realizing he was lucky to be alive, Lucas pushed himself into the arts and culture via photography, anthropology, and, eventually, film.

Unlike the 1997 theater-only trailer for *The Phantom Menace*, 2002's *Star Wars Episode II: Attack of the Clones* preview premiered on the Fox TV network between an episode of *Malcolm in the Middle* and *The X-Files*. It ran on *StarWars.com* the next day, kicking off the tradition of watching *Star Wars* trailers on the Internet.

Before *Star Wars*, Lucas had originally planned to do another movie: *Apocalypse Now*. He had first developed the Vietnam War–set drama with screenwriter John Milius in the late '60s, and intended to shoot it guerrilla-documentary style in 16mm. Francis Ford Coppola, who had the rights to Milius' script, ultimately took the idea back from Lucas and filmed it himself as a big-budget extravaganza.

Lucas was so concerned about the violence in *Star Wars Episode V: The Empire Strikes Back* that he consulted child psychologists before he finished filming. He was most worried about the dark ending, which included a severely injured Luke Skywalker, a frozen Han Solo, and a crippled Rebellion force. According to Lucas, experts said kids would be able to process the drama—even if the good guys didn't win until the next movie years later.

Critics have attacked *Star Wars* dialogue, particularly in the second trilogy, but Lucas himself admits that he is a terrible writer and struggled in English classes throughout college. Despite this, Lucas officially worked with collaborators only on the screenplays for *Star Wars Episode II: Attack of the Clones* (with Jonathan Hales) *and Star Wars Episode VI: The Return of the Jedi* (with Lawrence Kasdan). For the remaining movies, he wrote the original stories and final screenplays.

Star Wars Episode VI: The Return of the Jedi was the first Star Wars film to be completely mastered in-house. In fact, Lucasfilm had grown large enough to do most of the work itself. The audio facilities and research eventually grew into the groundbreaking THX technology. THX focused on theater sound until the mid-'90s, then expanded into home-video systems. Unlike Dolby and other brands, THX isn't a specific sound system, but a seal of approval based on a respective sound system meeting a minimum set of quality standards.

To make the lightsaber sound, the effects team combined two noises: the hum of an old movie projector and a microphone getting feedback from a nearby television. In the 1970s, televisions were much more sensitive to outside interference. For example, putting a magnet too close to a TV would cause temporary rainbow-like discolorations on the screen. Audio distortions also occurred with certain electronic sound equipment, and the *Star Wars* team was able to capture these odd noises to create the classic lightsaber sound.

Yoda in *Star Wars Episode V: The Empire Strikes Back* was essentially a hand puppet, which made it nearly impossible to film him running alongside Luke Skywalker during the Jedi-training sequence on the swamp planet Dagobah. Instead, Lucas and his team showed Yoda hanging onto Luke's back as he trained. (In reality, Hamill had the puppet stuffed in a backpack.)

Launching 21 years after the original trilogy, the second *Star Wars* trilogy depended more on CGI than real models, but Lucas still had to create elaborate, life-size sets on which actors could interact. Anything beyond the actors themselves and their costumes, however, was created with computer graphics.

⇒ Three ⇐

The number of Emmys won by *Star Wars: The Clone Wars*—two for Outstanding Animated Program and one to background key designer Justin Thompson for Outstanding Individual Achievement in Animation.

QUESTION:

In his first interview about it, how did George Lucas describe *Star Wars*?

QUESTION:

What was R2-D2 named after?

ANSWER:

A mixture of *Lawrence of Arabia*, the James Bond films, and *2001: A Space Odyssey*.

ANSWER:

Reel 2, Dialog 2, a sound-mixing reference George Lucas heard while he was editing *American Graffiti*.

The success of the animated *Star Wars: The Clone Wars* spin-off even surprised Lucasfilm. Launched in 2003, the Cartoon Network–helmed series lasted for two years and included 25 episodes. It was successful enough for Lucasfilm to launch another *Clone Wars* series, created by its in-house team, and a spin-off theatrical film in 2008.

Unlike every other film in the series, 2005's *Star Wars Episode III: Revenge of the Sith* was filmed entirely within a studio: Fox Studios Australia in Sydney. In comparison, 1977's *Star Wars Episode IV: A New Hope* was filmed on multiple continents.

QUESTION:

Which of the six *Star Wars* films did George Lucas *not* direct?

a. *Star Wars Episode I: The Phantom Menace*

b. *Star Wars Episode II: Attack of the Clones*

c. *Star Wars Episode III: Revenge of the Sith*

d. *Star Wars Episode IV: A New Hope*

e. *Star Wars Episode V: The Empire Strikes Back*

f. *Star Wars Episode VI: The Return of the Jedi*

ANSWER:

e. *Star Wars Episode V: The Empire Strikes Back*, and

f. *Star Wars Episode VI: The Return of the Jedi*

Irvin Kershner directed episode V, while Richard Marquand took the reins for episode VI.

After the release of his dark, cynical *THX 1138*, George Lucas was slammed from many corners for the film's bleak vision of a dehumanized future. This pushed him to bring a brighter attitude to his next science-fiction project. The stark good-and-evil characterizations of *Star Wars Episode IV: A New Hope* and the (spoiler alert!) rousing finale where the Rebellion defeats the Empire showed his response.

First appearing in *Star Wars Episode V: The Empire Strikes Back*, the Empire's massive armored personnel carriers, the AT-AT Walkers, were inspired by H. G. Wells' Martian-invasion novel *The War of the Worlds*. Lucas loved Wells' vision of aliens invading Earth via giant robotic spiders. He tried to create a similarly threatening feel with the Walkers, especially by making them tall enough for the landspeeders to weave through their legs.

TRUE OR FALSE?

The cartoon series *Star Wars: The Clone Wars* was directed by the guy behind *The Powerpuff Girls*.

TRUE.

Popular animator Genndy Tartakovsky also launched *The Powerpuff Girls*, *Samurai Jack*, and *Dexter's Laboratory*.

The lightsaber duels were inspired by turn-of-the-century cinema and classic Japanese swordsman techniques. The film element came from Errol Flynn's 1938 hit *The Adventures of Robin Hood* and other movies that created fast, intense swashbuckling scenes. There is also an homage to Kendo, the ancient Japanese martial art that favors accuracy over speed. Critics note that the earlier *Star Wars* movies lean toward slow, methodical jousting, while later films, like *Star Wars VI: The Return of the Jedi*, have faster-paced battles. The speed may also reflect the technology, which early on had a harder time handling the quick, neon lightsaber movements.

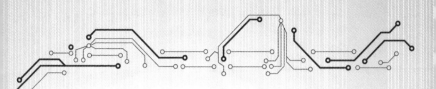

QUESTION:

Where did George Lucas attend school?

a. University of Southern California

b. University of California
   Santa Cruz

c. University of California
   Los Angeles

d. University of Phoenix

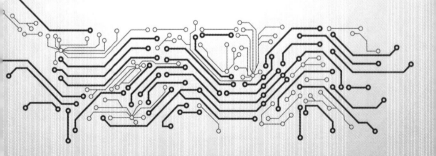

ANSWER:

a. University of Southern California

USC became a breeding ground for the next generation of '70s filmmakers, including Lucas' pal Francis Ford Coppola. Steven Spielberg applied to, and was rejected by, USC twice, but it gave him an honorary degree in 1994.

Lucasfilm announced that it would re-release all six films in 3D, beginning with *Star Wars Episode I: The Phantom Menace* in 2013. This project was put on hold, however, after lackluster box office results for the first film.

Although the Star Wars series was greatly inspired by Japanese director Akira Kurosawa, Lucas could not easily access Kurosawa's films. Unlike today, Lucas could not watch home videos or online clips to refresh his memory of particular scenes. He had to get Kurosawa's plot details from Donald Richie's classic book, *The Films of Akira Kurosawa*.

The original trilogy proved much stronger at the Oscars than its follow-up:

- *Star Wars Episode I: The Phantom Menace*: no wins from 3 nominations

- *Star Wars Episode II: Attack of the Clones*: no wins from 1 nomination

- *Star Wars Episode III: Revenge of the Sith*: no wins from 1 nomination

- *Star Wars Episode IV: A New Hope*: 7 wins from 11 nominations

- *Star Wars Episode V: The Empire Strikes Back*: 2 wins from 4 nominations

- *Star Wars Episode VI: The Return of the Jedi*: 1 win from 5 nominations

Star Wars Episode II: Attack of the Clones was one of the first movies to be filmed entirely using high-definition 24p digital technology (recording high-resolution shots 24 times per second, a remarkable technological feat at the time). Attack of the Clones required six large, very expensive 24p devices to shoot. Released in 2002, it was well ahead of the high-definition theater and television boom that would happen later in the decade.

The 1983 Star Wars arcade game was a massive hit despite the technical limitations of the time. The game focused on the fast-paced Death Star attack from *Star Wars Episode IV: A New Hope*, but there was a problem: Arcade technology could handle either complex graphics or fast visuals, but not both. Game developers at Atari used an older technique, called vector graphics, that created all the graphics out of straight lines. The intense, surreal effect helped Star Wars Arcade stand out in the arcade and gave gamers a fast, visually striking experience equal to the original movie. The classic Star Wars Arcade is still revered today, showing up on lists as one of the greatest arcade games of all time.

QUESTION:

What did George Lucas study as an undergraduate?

a. Music
b. Anthropology
c. Archaeology
d. Car mechanics

ANSWER:

b. Anthropology

Lucas' fascination with the history of human societies and cultural archetypes heavily influenced his writing of the *Star Wars* films. He famously studied the writings of Joseph Campbell, whose books on mythology—particularly *The Hero with a Thousand Faces*—were critical to the storyline of episodes like *The Empire Strikes Back*.

Star Wars may not have happened without Dennis Hopper's surprise hit *Easy Rider*. The 1969 biker film showed Hollywood studios that counterculture, youth-focused movies were box-office gold. (Warren Beatty's ultra-violent *Bonnie and Clyde* and the sexy Dustin Hoffman vehicle *The Graduate*, both released in 1967, also did well, but investors wouldn't take the trend seriously until later.) Warner Bros. in particular began looking for young, edgy auteurs, offering the just-graduated George Lucas and his mentor Francis Ford Coppola a multifilm deal. The deal eventually fell through, but it opened the doors to the 20th Century Fox offer that would bring about *Star Wars*.

Launched in winter 2005, Wookieepedia: The Star Wars Wiki may be the biggest archive of Star Wars details on the web. Founders Chad Barbry and Steven Greenwood have helped amass more than 100,000 articles about the Star Wars universe. A second great resource is the Lucasfilm-sanctioned *StarWars.com*, which packs official interviews, historical information, and, most notably, any breaking Star Wars news. Both are worth a visit after enjoying this book.

Much to the chagrin of fans, Lucas made the most changes in the Special Edition of *Star Wars Episode IV: A New Hope*, rather than in V and VI. He says it made sense because the technology was the oldest in the first film and, therefore, the 1977 movie needed the biggest visual update 20 years later. The Special Edition of *A New Hope* included computer-generated backgrounds, a completely CGI scene between Han Solo and a smaller Jabba the Hutt, and the infamous "Greedo Shoots First" revamp.

$10,000,000,000+

As of Spring 2013,
the total estimated amount
of money spent by consumers
on Star Wars toys.

George Lucas is a big fan of legendary Japanese director Akira Kurosawa (1910–1998), whose body of work left an indelible mark on *Star Wars Episode IV: A New Hope*. The director of *Rashomon* and *The Seven Samurai* was known for explaining less and showing more—to paraphrase Lucas, Kurosawa would throw the film audience in the middle of a scenario and trust that it would pick up quickly on what was happening.

The original *Star Wars* uses the same technique, putting the audience literally in the middle of the six-film series. Most notably, Kurosawa's movies often followed minor characters to tell the story, perhaps to give more objectivity for the audience. Lucas followed suit, focusing most of the movie on two seemingly random characters: R2-D2 and C-3PO. He had no idea the duo would become some of the most beloved characters in the series, and later spawn their own comics, books, and other stories.

In the United States, *Star Wars* is the second-biggest box office hit ever, with a total take for *Episode IV: A New Hope* pegged at $460,998,007. But that's in 1977 dollars. Adjusted for 2013 inflation, it raked in $1,433,862,700. The king of the American box office remains 1939's *Gone With the Wind*, which brought in the 2013 equivalent of $1,626,459,200. (Unadjusted, the southern epic brought in $198,679,459, a decent number even by today's standards.)

At number 12 is *Episode V: The Empire Strikes Back*, with $790,354,100, or $290,475,067 in 1980 rates. *Episode VI: Return of the Jedi* and *Episode I: The Phantom Menace* are back to back at numbers 15 and 16, pulling in $757,178,300 ($309 million in 1983) and $727,012,200 ($475 million in 1999). Further down the list at number 60 is *Episode III: Revenge of the Sith*, with $477,562,900 ($380 million in 2005). The most critically bashed *Episode II: Attack of the Clones*, is last at number 87, with $430,421,200 ($311 million in 2002).

When George Lucas first started working on *Star Wars*, he used free association to name his characters. The first name he came up with? "Emperor Ford Xerxes XII," who would become Alexander Xerxes XII, the Emperor of Decente, and, in the final manuscript, Emperor Palpatine.

The Death Star is often talked about in the singular, but there are actually three within the timeline of the two *Star Wars* trilogies. The first was destroyed by Luke Skywalker in *Star Wars Episode IV: A New Hope* and had a diameter of 160 kilometers, or about 100 miles across. Pretty small! Think about the hour and a half it would take to drive that same distance at 60 mph. In comparison, Earth itself is just under 13,000 kilometers, or about 8,000 miles across.

The second Death Star was much bigger, measuring 900 kilometers, or about 560 miles across. At six times the size of the first Death Star, it's safe to assume that the original was just a prototype for the big one to come later. Lando Calrissian destroyed the second Death Star in *Star Wars Episode VI: The Return of the Jedi*. However, parallel Star Wars stories reference a third Death Star that was annihilated by another part of the Rebel Alliance at the same time Calrissian sunk the second one.

QUESTION:

Which is *not* a LEGO Star Wars video game?

a. **LEGO Star Wars: The Complete Saga**

b. **LEGO Star Wars III: The Clone Wars**

c. **LEGO Star Wars: The Video Game**

d. **LEGO Star Wars: Jar Jar Binks Pinball**

ANSWER:

d. LEGO Star Wars: Jar Jar Binks Pinball

The first game—LEGO Star Wars: The Video Game— was released in 2005. Lucasfilm and LEGO began developing Star Wars-themed toys in 1999. In 2008, almost 15 million Star Wars LEGO box sets were sold, which breaks down to 28 every minute.

Initially created just for *Star Wars*, Lucas' special effects-studio Industrial Light and Magic became a multimillion-dollar stand-alone studio contributing to dozens of blockbuster, groundbreaking films, including:

- *E.T.: The Extra-Terrestrial* (1982)
- *Terminator 2: Judgment Day* (1991)
- *Forrest Gump* (1994)
- *Toy Story* (1995)
- *Titanic* (1997)
- *Pirates of the Caribbean: The Curse of the Black Pearl* (2003)
- *Transformers* (2007)
- *Avatar* (2009)

Before *Star Wars*, George Lucas tried to bring another space opera to film: *Flash Gordon*. He approached comic company King Features about buying the rights, but it jacked up the price after Lucas' perceived interest and went way out of his price range. After producer Dino DeLaurentis grabbed the rights, Lucas decided to write his own space opera.

Lucas, of course, ended up having the last laugh. DeLaurentis' campy *Flash Gordon* got mixed reviews and hauled in an estimated $27 million worldwide, only a few million more than its reported $20 million budget. The original *Star Wars* had just over half of Flash Gordon's budget (without the hefty licensing fee) and brought in nearly half a billion dollars.

The movie misstep didn't seem to hurt *Flash Gordon*'s popularity. Since then, the story has been told in TV animated specials, a SyFy Channel live-action series, and dozens of new comic books.

QUESTION:

When *Star Wars* started filming, George Lucas had already worked with Harrison Ford in what movie?

ANSWER:

Ford appeared in Lucas' first hit, 1973's *American Graffiti*. He played Bob Falfa, an aggressive out-of-town hot rodder looking to race in Modesto, California. The following year, Ford scored a role in Francis Ford Coppola's *The Conversation*.

The Star Wars series isn't known for having many human female characters, but three of the most notable were cut from *Star Wars Episode VI: The Return of the Jedi*. All are A-wing pilots, including an older woman who looks like she's in her sixties. No one has revealed why the three pilots weren't included in the theatrical release, but Lucas added their scenes as extras to later home editions.

Female heroines and villains are much more prominent in the expanded Star Wars universe described in countless comics and books. The dozens of strong women are narrowed down to a few in the movies, including the powerful blue Jedi Guardian Aayla Secura featured in *Star Wars Episode II: Attack of the Clones* and *Star Wars: The Clone Wars*, and, of course, hero and future Jedi Princess Leia Organa.

R2-D2 is the Swiss Army knife of droids, with abilities including:

- Underwater mode with periscope
- Holoprojector
- Lightsaber compartment
- Smoke screen gun
- Electric shock arm
- Flea remover

QUESTION:

Midichlorians explain what Star Wars phenomenon?

a. The lightsaber

b. The Force

c. Warp speed

d. Oxygen on foreign planets

ANSWER:

b. The Force

Midichlorians are bacteria found in the bloodstream that emanate through the skin. The Force was originally defined as a focused belief, akin to a heightened meditation, but Lucas added the midichlorian concept in the second trilogy. Fans had a strong, generally negative reaction, since it turned the Force into a physical, hereditary concept, rather than a pseudo-spiritual one.

Writing the first *Star Wars* script was far from an easy process for George Lucas. According to several reports, he had crippling writers' block. Lucas kept himself locked in his writing room for days and dealt with regular headaches, stomach issues, and chest pains. It took him a year to write it.

George Lucas' *Star Wars* deal didn't come together until a few weeks after *American Graffiti* was released. Luckily, the low-budget film was a big hit, earning more than $100 million at the box office. Lucas used his resulting clout with 20th Century Fox to get $50,000 for the *Star Wars* manuscript and $100,000 to direct it. This was still a small sum compared to more popular directors, but not nearly as small as the $20,000 he got for *American Graffiti*. It all worked out, as *American Graffiti*'s profits eventually made Lucas a millionaire.

By early 2013, Lucas was worth an estimated $3.2 billion. Most of his wealth came from the *Star Wars* films and, most important, Star Wars–related merchandise like toys, clothing, and music. His net worth also got a boost from selling Lucasfilm to Disney for $4.08 billion in October 2012.

TRUE OR FALSE?

The rarest Star Wars trading card shows C-3PO in a very "excited" position.

TRUE.

Known by collectors as the "207 error card," the image on the C-3PO trading card includes an extra metal pole near the robot's legs.

TRUE OR FALSE?

The Ewok language is based on a Yucatán dialect.

FALSE.

It is based on a rare Asian language in central China. The primary tune the Ewoks hum throughout episode VI was inspired by an old Chinese folk song.

QUESTION:

Every *Star Wars* film has an MPAA rating of PG, except for which PG-13 movie?

   a. *Star Wars Episode III: Revenge of the Sith*

   b. *Star Wars Episode IV: A New Hope*

   c. *Star Wars Episode V: The Empire Strikes Back*

   d. *Star Wars Episode I: The Phantom Menace*

ANSWER:

a. *Star Wars Episode III: Revenge of the Sith*

Lucas told *60 Minutes* he wouldn't take a 5- or 6-year-old to the film. He said the film would show Anakin making "a pact with the devil.... The film is more dark ... more emotional. It's much more of a tragedy."

Lucas' inspiration for Chewbacca came from his pet dog. According to the director, Lucas watched his hirsute canine rise to attention in the passenger seat of his car and envisioned a tall, hairy, human-like creature. The onscreen version ended up towering over the rest of the cast—actor Peter Mayhew, who played Chewbacca in all of the films, stood at 7'3" before donning the costume. Lucas' dog contributed to another franchise: Its name, Indiana, was lent to the hero of the next non-*Star Wars* film Lucas produced, 1981's *Raiders of the Lost Ark*. In a wink to real life, in 1989's *Indiana Jones and the Last Crusade* Indy's father chides him for taking the nickname: "We named the dog Indiana!"

The Star Wars universe has inspired many board games, including:

- Monopoly Star Wars Original Trilogy Edition (1997)

- Trivial Pursuit—Star Wars Classic Trilogy Collector's Edition (1997)

- The Game of Life: Star Wars—Jedi's Path (2002)

- Stratego Star Wars Edition (2005)

- Star Wars Risk: The Clone Wars Edition (2005) and Risk: Star Wars Original Trilogy Edition (2006)

- Operation Star Wars Edition (2011)

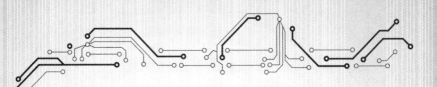

QUESTION:

In *Star Wars Episode V: The Empire Strikes Back*, Chewbacca crying at the disassembled head of C-3PO was inspired by which Shakespeare play?

a. *Hamlet*

b. *Romeo and Juliet*

c. *The Tempest*

d. *The Merchant of Venice*

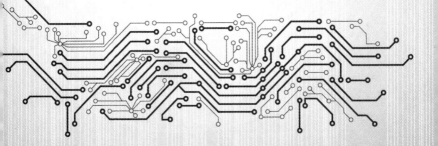

ANSWER:

a. *Hamlet*

Director Irvin Kershner loved adding the literary reference, but later said he was confident most viewers weren't expecting, and therefore didn't get, a random Shakespeare ode in the middle of a space opera.

During the 2011 Super Bowl, Volkswagen showed one of the most popular ads of all time. A young boy in a Darth Vader Halloween outfit walks around his family's house trying to use the Force to move objects. Nothing works. In a last-ditch effort, he goes out to his dad's car, stretches out his arms, and strains to move the two-ton Volkswagen. Suddenly, the car engine revs! The boy stops in shock, convinced he has tapped his hidden power, while his father aims the remote key at the car from the kitchen window. Since then, *The Force: Volkswagen Commercial* has racked up more than 56 million views on YouTube.

The American Film Institute celebrated a century of modern film by making several lists, including the Top 100 Heroes and Villains of all time. *Star Wars* was strong on the heroes list, with Han Solo at number 14 and Obi-Wan Kenobi at number 37. Darth Vader was the only bad guy from the franchise to make the list, but he was also the highest-ranked Star Wars character, earning the third-best movie villain of all time.

TRUE OR FALSE?

The foghorn noises in Lando's Cloud City are from Nigerian tugboats.

FALSE.

The sounds heard in *Star Wars V: The Empire Strikes Back* were recorded off boats in the San Francisco Bay near Skywalker Ranch.

Every film in both *Star Wars* trilogies was released within days of May 14, George Lucas' birthday:

- *Star Wars Episode IV: A New Hope*: May 25, 1977

- *Star Wars Episode V: The Empire Strikes Back*: May 21, 1980

- *Star Wars Episode VI: The Return of the Jedi*: May 25, 1983

- *Star Wars Episode I: The Phantom Menace*: May 19, 1999

- *Star Wars Episode II: Attack of the Clones*: May 16, 2002

- *Star Wars Episode III: Revenge of the Sith*: May 19, 2005

QUESTION:

What song *wasn't* featured on the 1980 Star Wars holiday album *Christmas In the Stars*?

a. "R2-D2 We Wish You a Merry Christmas"

b. "What Can You Get a Wookie for Christmas (When He Already Owns a Comb?)"

c. "The Death Star is Our North Star"

d. "Sleigh Ride"

ANSWER:

c. "The Death Star is Our North Star"

QUESTION:

The animated *Star Wars: The Clone Wars* fills the gap between which set of films?

a. *Star Wars Episode I: The Phantom Menace* and *Star Wars Episode II: Attack of the Clones*

b. *Star Wars Episode II: Attack of the Clones* and *Star Wars Episode III: Revenge of the Sith*

c. *Star Wars Episode IV: A New Hope* and *Star Wars Episode V: The Empire Strikes Back*

d. Before *Star Wars Episode I: The Phantom Menace*

ANSWER:

b. *Star Wars Episode II: Attack of the Clones* and *Star Wars Episode III: Revenge of the Sith*

QUESTION:

Star Wars Episode IV: A New Hope is arguably a remake of Akira Kurasowa's 1958 film *The Hidden Fortress*. What other non-Japanese films did the legendary Kurosawa inspire?

ANSWER:

The Seven Samurai (1954) became the Yul Brynner and Steve McQueen Western *The Magnificent Seven* (1960).

Rashomon (1950) became the Paul Newman drama *The Outrage* (1964).

Yojimbo (1961) became the Clint Eastwood spaghetti western *A Fistful of Dollars* (1964).

QUESTION:

What Francis Ford Coppola film was Lucas' big break?

    a. *The Conversation*

    b. *Finian's Rainbow*

    c. *Apocalypse Now*

    d. *The Godfather*

ANSWER:

b. *Finian's Rainbow*

Coppola hired Lucas to be an administrative assistant on this 1968 Fred Astaire musical, and then as production assistant on his next film, *The Rain People* (Lucas' wife, Marcia, worked as assistant editor).

DAMON BROWN

ABOUT THE AUTHOR

Damon Brown is the author of several pop culture titles, most notably the TED Book *Our Virtual Shadow: Why We are Obsessed with Documenting Our Lives Online*, the coffee-table book *Playboy's Greatest Covers*, and the critically acclaimed *Porn & Pong: How Grand Theft Auto, Tomb Raider and Other Sexy Games Changed Our Culture*. He is also the co-founder of Quote UnQuote, an app that lets you document interesting things you hear people say. He has written for *Playboy*, *New York Post*, and CNN. You can catch him online at *www.damonbrown.net* or discussing pop culture on Twitter at @browndamon.

REFERENCES

Easy Riders, Raging Bulls by Peter Biskind

Star Wars: The Complete Saga (Blu-Ray)

The Secret History of Star Wars by Michael Kaminski

The People vs. George Lucas (DVD)

Wookieepedia: The Star Wars Wiki
(http://starwars.wikia.com/wiki/Main_Page)

The Official Star Wars Website
(http://starwars.com/)

Box Office Mojo
(http://boxofficemojo.com/)